Light Keepers

Be Thou an Example

Songs for Youth Songbook

Light Keepers

Be Thou an Example
Songs for Youth Songbook

Jenny Phillips

SHADOW MOUNTAIN RECORDS
The premier record label of Deseret Book Company

P.O. Box 30178

Salt Lake City, UT 84130–0178

ISBN 978-1-60641-088-2

Printed in the United States of America
Artistic Printing, Salt Lake City, UT
10 9 8 7 6 5 4 3 2 1

Contents

PROGRAM INSTRUCTIONS

THE PROGRAM

Light Keepers is a musical program that can be performed by wards or stakes. This program celebrates the 2009 theme, "Be thou an example of the believers, in word, in conversation, in charity, in spirit, in faith, in purity" (1 Timothy 4:12). The program consists of six songs, live narration, and one recorded narration. This performance doesn't require any costumes, props, or scenery.

WHEN TO PERFORM THE PROGRAM

You can perform Light Keepers any time of the year as a ward or stake fireside, youth fireside, New Beginnings program, Young Women in Excellence program, girls' camp, or youth activity.

MAKING COPIES OF THE SCRIPT

You may make copies of the script without permission.

BULK CDS AND REHEARSAL SONGBOOK

To make rehearsing this program fit your budget, we offer bulk CDs (without the jewel case or CD booklet) for $3 each on www.JennyPhillips.com, or they can be requested from your local bookstore. These CDs are perfect to give out to the girls so that they can learn the music. They are also great to give out as gifts at your event. You can also download a free rehearsal songbook (includes melody and lyrics but not piano accompaniment) at JennyPhillips.com. You can make copies of the rehearsal songbook free of charge.

THE LENGTH OF THE PROGRAM

If followed exactly as outlined in the script, Light Keepers is about 50 minutes long. Without the optional youth testimonies the script is about 40 minutes long.

SHORTENING THE PROGRAM

You are welcome to skip any of the different sections of the program to shorten the program if needed.

You can still perform this program if you have a small youth group or don't want to put together a choir. Use the simplified script (available on pp. xiv–xvii of this songbook) to perform the program with as little as one female soloist and 2 narrators (no choir needed).

WHAT YOU NEED TO PERFORM THE PROGRAM

Accompaniment tracks or sheet music. You may use the accompaniment tracks included on the CD, use a pianist, or use a combination of the two.

Copyright permission. Sheet music for Light Keepers may not be copied without permission. You can purchase inexpensive copy permissions on JennyPhillips.com (from the main menu, click on "Buy Sheet Music/Copy Permissions). You may also download a free "Rehearsal Songbook" (melody lines and choir parts without piano accompaniment) on JennyPhillips.com. The "Rehearsal Songbook" may be copied without charge or permission. Burning copies of the CD or any portion of the CD is prohibited by law. Visit JennyPhillips.com and select "Bulk Orders" to buy the CDs for $3 each in packs of five. The bulk order CDs include all the songs and accompaniment tracks, but come in a paper slip-sleeve and do not include the CD booklet.

A sound system. Your church should have microphones and microphone hook-ups in the cultural hall. You will also need a way to play the minus tracks CD, either with a borrowed or rented sound system, or a nice portable stereo.

Singers. There are two songs with choir parts, and the rest are solos or solos with optional small choir parts. You could perform the choir songs with as few as four people, or you can have as many people as you want in the choir. We suggest that you have at least ten members of the choir. You can use as many or as few soloists as you want. Each song does not need to be performed with a different soloist. All songs are designed to be sung by young women, but "Fit for His Kingdom," has male back-up parts. If you do not have any male singers, you can use the instrumental track for "Fit for His Kingdom," that has the male backup recorded on it. Programs where the adult leaders sing all or some of the solo songs have worked well also.

TIPS/IDEAS

- If you want to perform the program, but you don't have a very musical ward or stake you could follow the simplified version of the script which is available on pp. xiv–xvii of this songbook.
- You could end with a talk by your bishop, stake president, or young women's president, or you could end with a youth testimony meeting.
- Visit JennyPhillips.com to download a free book called *102 Activities for Youth: Using the 2009 Theme* for decoration ideas, recipes, activities, themes, and more for New Beginnings, Girls' Camps, Young Women in Excellence, youth conference, and weekly activities.

DOWNLOADS AND HELPS

On JennyPhillips.com, you can download (go to "Free Downloads"):

- Posters
- Invitations
- Programs

Be Thou an Example

Script by Jenny Phillips

SONG ORDER:

Lighthouse in the Night (female soloist and choir)

Fit for His Kingdom (female soloist with optional male backup)

Firm in the Faith (female soloist with optional female choir backup)

Light Keeper (female soloist with optional choir)

He Is the Way (female soloist)

Hold Our Torches High (female choir or male/female choir)

NARRATOR #1:

1 Timothy 4:12: "Be thou an example of the believers, in word, in conversation, in charity, in spirit, in faith, in purity."

NARRATOR #2:

President Thomas S. Monson said: "You are an example of righteousness in a world which desperately needs your influence and your strength. . . . Today, permissiveness, immorality, pornography, and the power of peer pressure cause many to be tossed on a sea of sin and crushed on the jagged reefs of lost opportunities, forfeited blessings, and shattered dreams. . . . You can share your testimony in many ways—by the words you speak, by the example you set, by the manner in which you live your life" ("Be Thou an Example," *Ensign,* May 2005, 112, 115).

YOUTH TESTIMONIES

Choose two young women to share a two-minute testimony on "the impact of an example." They can talk about how someone else's example affected them, or how someone was affected by their example. Remind the young women to keep it short and make sure they don't go over two minutes. Make sure their example isn't someone in the scriptures, as there will be scriptural examples later in the program.

Youth #1: ____________________________________

Youth #2: ____________________________________

NARRATOR #2:

When you live the commandments and standards of the gospel and continually nourish your spirit, you are like a light that cuts through the mists of darkness in the world, illuminating the night, and leading the way to safety. People who are searching will be attracted to that light. You can be a great influence on those around you.

Henry B. Eyring said: "When you walk in the light, you will feel at that moment some of the warmth and the happiness that will finally be yours when you are welcomed home again with the hundreds and perhaps thousands of others whom you will bring with you, who have walked in the light because you did" ("Walk in the Light," *Ensign,* May 2008, 125).

PERFORM SONG: "Lighthouse in the Night"

[Female soloist and choir]

NARRATOR #1:

Brigham Young said, "Cleave to light and intelligence with all your hearts . . . that you may be prepared to preserve your identity" (Brigham Young, *Journal of Discourses* 6:333).

NARRATOR #2:

That knowledge of who you are can give you the courage and the strength to rise up and shine your light in this world. You are not simply a mortal being. You are a child of the almighty God. You are a righteous spirit that has existed for ages. You fought for truth, and you sided with God before this life. You earned the blessing to come to this earth. Henry B. Eyring said: "You are remarkable, even among those who chose right in the contest in the spirit world . . . among the billions of Heavenly Father's children now living, you were privileged to find the gospel of Jesus Christ and His true Church" ("Walk in the Light," *Ensign,* May 2008, 123).

It is so easy to lose the eternal picture—to become focused on the here and now; to be content to take the easy road of pleasure; and to swear allegiance to the side that we once fought against. But when we are obedient to the gospel and continually nourish our spirits, there is a light that illuminates the darkness, and our spiritual eyes are able to see the eternal picture. With our premortal life, mortal life, and post-mortal life all before our eyes, we begin to realize how incredibly important this probationary time on earth is.

Our all-powerful God who created the planets, the stars, and every living thing has a fulness of glory, a fulness of joy, a fulness of life, a fulness of light and knowledge. We cannot comprehend the beauty and the joy that He posseses. But all He has, every part of His kingdom, He offers to us. He created us that we might have joy. And He wants us to have a fulness of life and light. He wants us to be like Him. If we could really understand what it is He offers us, and keep it in our minds continually, there would be nothing we wouldn't do to follow Him. We would realize that a mere seventy or eighty years on this earth will determine what our existence will be like for all eternity.

We prepared for this life. We yearned for it. Oh, how we must've prayed that we would never lose sight of why we were on the earth. Our eyes should be riveted on the pathway to the celestial kingdom.

PERFORM SONG: "Fit for His Kingdom"

[Female soloist and optional male backup]

NARRATOR #1:

The Lord knew we would live on the earth at a time when we would be flooded with wrong examples. That is one of the reasons that the scriptures are so vital to our journey. They are filled with examples of men and women who were firm in their faith.

YOUTH TESTIMONIES ON SCRIPTURE EXAMPLES

Choose two young women to share a two-minute testimony on how the example of someone in the scriptures has affected their life. It doesn't have to be a particular incident—it could also be the overall way they have been affected by the example. Remind the youth to keep it short and make sure they don't go over two minutes.

Youth #1: ____

Youth #2: ____

NARRATOR #2:

When we keep the mighty examples contained in the scriptures before our eyes continually, our lives change. We become what we think about. And we think about what we read, and hear, and see. We become like those that we strive to emulate. Ezra Taft Benson said: "God uses the power of the word of the Book of Mormon as an instrument to change people's lives: 'As the preaching of the word had a great tendency to lead the people to do that which was just—yea, it had had more powerful effect upon the minds of the people than the sword, or anything else, which had happened unto them' (Alma 31:5)" (*A Witness and a Warning* [Salt Lake City: Deseret Book, 1988], 32).

PERFORM SONG: "FIRM IN THE FAITH"

[Female soloist and optional female choir backup]

NARRATOR #3:

Light and darkness cannot occupy the same space at the same time. This is both a physical and a spiritual law. Light is always stronger than darkness. Wherever light is, darkness has to flee.

When we carry spiritual light inside us, we will have an influence for good on everyone we come in contact with. The adversary knows the powerful impact that one light keeper can have on the world around them. He would do anything to dim the light of one faithful light keeper. In today's world, he whispers that wearing immodest clothing is not a big deal. He carefully keeps us from realizing the light that we lose from dressing immodestly.

L. Tom Perry said: "The way we dress is usually a good indicator of how we will act" ("'Train Up a Child,'" *Ensign,* November 1988, 75). Dressing modestly is an important part of keeping the light of the Spirit in our lives. You cannot dress immodestly and keep the Spirit fully in your life. You will not have the brightness of the Spirit in your countenance, and your vision will be darkened. Without the Spirit you be walking in darkness. In the Doctrine and Covenants it says: "If you keep not my commandments, the love of the Father shall not continue with you, therefore you shall walk in darkness" (D&C 95:12). When we dress immodestly, we bring darkness into other lives by inviting impure thoughts and causing others to lose the spirit. With the knowledge that we have, we should be keepers of light and not spreaders of darkness.

NARRATOR #1:

When Jesus was tempted by Satan, he said "Get thee behind me, Satan." When we are tempted to participate in immorality or pornography, we should follow the Savior's example, and immediately put those temptations behind us, that they may not be before our eyes or in our minds or on our pathway.

The Lord knows how hard it is to live a clean life in today's world. He understands on a perfect level what you are facing in your life, and how strong temptation can be. He knows because He has suffered all the temptations you face. And He overcame them all, and He knows how to help you overcome them. You may have times where you feel like you stand alone by living the standards of the church, but you can be assured that the Savior supports those who follow His counsel. His promises to those who trust Him are incredible. Just as the adversary would do anything to destroy that light in you and make you lose your divine potential, the Savior would do anything to increase your light and shape you into something strong and eternally beautiful and blessed.

It will take a lot of trust in the Savior to live a clean life today. But this life is all about trusting the Savior. This life is based on the principle of faith. Do you have faith in His counsel? Will you follow Him, even when it's hard? This is what you came here to prove. The Savior Jesus Christ is the truest and dearest friend you will ever have in this life. He can always be trusted. His promises are sure. Living a life of modesty and chastity is worth any price that it takes. If we really understood the value of our purity, we would guard it with our lives. The purity inside us is the very fountain of our light and of the life of our spirit. Immodesty, pornography, and sexual sin destroy life and light and spirit. No matter how appealing Satan can make these things appear, they lead to destruction. The prince of darkness, who wants nothing more than to destroy all good in you, will try with all his power and might to get you to be involved in immodesty, pornography, and sexual sin. He has taken the light from so many on the earth through these things. Oh, how our Heavenly Father needs your strength. How he needs you to stay clean. You have a knowledge of the truth. As the 2,000 stripling warriors, you have been taught to keep the commandments of God. As you stand up to the adversary and cleave to the light of your Father, you will become a force for good. The light inside you will grow and will shine from your countenance. Your example of purity will dispel darkness from around you, because darkness cannot be where light is.

Don't be afraid to be different from the world. Don't be afraid to be a witness at all times, and in all things, and in all places. Your decisions about modesty and morality are shaping your eternal destiny. This is your time. This is your day. You were created to be greater than the lowly things of this world. You are divine. You are youth of the noble birthright. You are a light keeper.

PERFORM SONG: "Light Keeper"

[Female soloist and optional female choir backup]

NARRATOR #2:

When the apostle Paul said, "Be thou an example of the believers" (1 Timothy 4:12), he was writing to a faithful young missionary named Timothy.

As the Lord's youth in these latter days we can all be examples of the believers, like that young missionary, Timothy. We know the truth. We have the fulness of the everlasting gospel in our midst. By the words we speak, by living in purity, by our faith, by the Spirit we carry, through our love and our charity, our examples will lead men to peace and truth and the safety of the gospel of Jesus Christ.

In D&C Section 123 it says: "For there are many yet on the earth . . . who are only kept from the truth because they know not where to find it—Therefore, that we should waste and wear out our lives in bringing to light all the hidden things of darkness, wherein we know them" (vv. 12–13).

PERFORM SONG: "He Is the Way"

[Female soloist]

PLAY THE RECORDED NARRATION "The Example of Jesus Christ":

**This recorded narration is track #14 on the CD* Light Keepers.

**If you don't play this narration, you may read this narration. It can be downloaded for free on JennyPhillips.com (go to "Free Downloads").*

**In place of this narration (played or read), you can have a leader or a youth give their testimony about Christ being the greatest example of all.*

PERFORM SONG: "Hold Our Torches High"

[Female or male/female choir]

Light Keepers

Be Thou an Example

Simplified Script

by Jenny Phillips

**This script is designed for wards or branches that are small or do not have enough musical talent to perform the full program.*

**This program can be performed with as little as one female soloist.*

SONG ORDER:

Lighthouse in the Night (female soloist and choir)

Firm in the Faith (female soloist with optional female choir backup)

Light Keeper (female soloist with optional choir)

NARRATOR #1:

1 Timothy 4:12: " Be thou an example of the believers, in word, in conversation, in charity, in spirit, in faith, in purity."

NARRATOR #2:

President Thomas S. Monson said: "You are an example of righteousness in a world which desperately needs your influence and your strength. . . . Today, permissiveness, immorality, pornography, and the power of peer pressure cause many to be tossed on a sea of sin and crushed on the jagged reefs of lost opportunities, forfeited blessings, and shattered dreams. . . . You can share your testimony in many ways—by the words you speak, by the example you set, by the manner in which you live your life" ("Be Thou an Example," *Ensign,* May 2005, 112, 115).

YOUTH TESTIMONIES

Choose two young women to share a two-minute testimony on "the impact of an example." They can talk about how someone else's example affected them, or how someone was affected by their example. Remind the young women to keep it short and make sure they don't go over two minutes. Make sure their example isn't someone in the scriptures, as there will be scriptural examples later in the program.

Youth #1: ____

Youth #2: ____

NARRATOR #3:

When you live the commandments and standards of the gospel and continually nourish your spirit, you are like a light that cuts through the mists of darkness in the world, illuminating the night, and leading the way to safety. People who are searching will be attracted to that light. You can be a great influence on those around you.

Henry B. Eyring said: "When you walk in the light, you will feel at that moment some of the warmth and the happiness that will finally be yours when you are welcomed home again with the hundreds and perhaps thousands of others whom you will bring with you, who have walked in the light because you did" ("Walk in the Light," *Ensign,* May 2008, 125).

PERFORM SONG: "Lighthouse in the Night"

[Female soloist and choir]

NARRATOR #1:
The Lord knew we would live on the earth at a time when we would be flooded with the wrong examples. That is one of the reasons that the scriptures are so vital to our journey. They are filled with examples of men and women who were firm in their faith.

YOUTH TESTIMONIES ON SCRIPTURE EXAMPLES

Choose two young women to share a two-minute testimony on how the example of someone in the scriptures has affected their life. It doesn't have to be a particular incident—it could also be the overall way they have been affected by the example. Remind the youth to keep it short and make sure they don't go over two minutes.

Youth #1: ________________________________

Youth #2: ________________________________

NARRATOR #2:

When we keep the mighty examples contained in the scriptures before our eyes continually, our lives change. We become what we think about. And we think about what we read, and hear, and see. We become like those that we strive to emulate. Ezra Taft Benson said: "God uses the power of the word of the Book of Mormon as an instrument to change people's lives: 'As the preaching of the word had a great tendency to lead the people to do that which was just—yea, it had had more powerful effect upon the minds of the people than the sword, or anything else, which had happened unto them' (Alma 31:5)" (*A Witness and a Warning* [Salt Lake City: Deseret Book, 1988], 32).

PERFORM SONG: "Firm in the Faith"

[Female soloist with optional female choir backup]

NARRATOR #3:

Light and darkness cannot occupy the same space at the same time. This is both a physical and a spiritual law. Light is always stronger than darkness. Wherever light is, darkness has to flee.

When we carry spiritual light inside us, we will have an influence for good on everyone we come in contact with. The adversary knows the powerful impact that one light keeper can have on the world around them. He would do anything to dim the light of one faithful light keeper. In today's world, he whispers that wearing immodest clothing is not a big deal. He carefully keeps us from realizing the light that we lose from dressing immodestly.

L. Tom Perry said: "The way we dress is usually a good indicator of how we will act" ("'Train Up a Child,'" *Ensign,* November 1988, 75). Dressing modestly is an important part of keeping the light of the Spirit in our lives. You cannot dress immodestly and keep the Spirit fully in your life. You will not have the brightness of the Spirit in your countenance, and your vision will be darkened. Without the Spirit you be walking in darkness. In the Doctrine and Covenants it says: "If you keep not my commandments, the love of the Father shall not continue with you, therefore you shall walk in darkness" (D&C 95:12).

When we dress immodestly, we bring darkness into other lives by inviting impure thoughts and causing others to lose the spirit. With the knowledge that we have, we should be keepers of light and not spreaders of darkness.

NARRATOR #1:

When Jesus was tempted by Satan, he said "Get thee behind me, Satan." When we are tempted to participate in immorality or pornography, we should follow the Savior's example, and immediately put those temptations behind us, that they may not be before our eyes or in our minds or on our pathway.

The Lord knows how hard it is to live a clean life in today's world. He understands on a perfect level what you are facing in your life, and how strong temptation can be. He knows because He has suffered all the temptations you face. And He overcame them all, and He knows how to help you overcome them. You may have times where you feel like you stand alone by living the standards of the church, but you can be assured that the Savior supports those who follow His counsel. His promises to those who trust Him are incredible. Just as the adversary would do anything to destroy that light in you and make you lose your divine potential, the Savior would do anything to increase your light and shape you into something strong and eternally beautiful and blessed.

It will take a lot of trust in the Savior to live a clean life today. But this life is all about trusting the Savior. This life is based on the principle of faith. Do you have faith in His counsel? Will you follow Him, even when it's hard? This is what you came here to prove. The Savior Jesus Christ is the truest and dearest friend you will ever have in this life. He can always be trusted. His promises are sure. Living a life of modesty and chastity is worth any price that it takes. If we really understood the value of our purity, we would guard it with our lives. The purity inside us is the very fountain of our light and of the life of our spirit. Immodesty, pornography, and sexual sin destroy life and light and spirit. No matter how appealing Satan can make these things appear, they lead to destruction. The prince of darkness, who wants nothing more than to destroy all good in you, will try with all his power and might to get you to be involved in immodesty, pornography, and sexual sin. He has taken the light from so many on the earth through these things. Oh, how our Heavenly Father needs your strength. How he needs you to stay clean. You have a knowledge of the truth. As the 2,000 stripling warriors, you have been taught to keep the commandments of God. As you stand up to the adversary and cleave to the light of your Father, you will become a force for good. The light inside you will grow and will shine from your countenance. Your example of purity will dispel darkness from around you, because darkness cannot be where light is.

Don't be afraid to be different from the world. Don't be afraid to be a witness at all times, and in all things, and in all places. Your decisions about modesty and morality are shaping your eternal destiny. This is your time. This is your day. You were created to be greater than the lowly things of this world. You are divine. You are youth of the noble birthright. You are a light keeper.

PERFORM SONG: "Light Keeper"

[Female soloist and optional female choir backup]

NARRATOR #2:

When the apostle Paul said, "Be thou an example of the believers" (1 Timothy 4:12), he was writing to a faithful young missionary named Timothy.

As the Lord's youth in these latter days we can all be examples of the believers, like that young missionary, Timothy. We know the truth. We have the fullness of the everlasting gospel in our midst. By the words we speak, by living in purity, by our faith, by the Spirit we carry, through our love and our charity, our examples will lead men to peace and truth and the safety of the gospel of Jesus Christ. Jesus Christ is the light that we shine. He was the greatest example of the believers.

PLAY THE RECORDED NARRATION "The Example of Jesus Christ":

**This recorded narration is track #14 on the CD* Light Keepers.

**If you don't play this narration, you may read this narration. It can be downloaded for free on JennyPhillips.com (go to "Free Downloads").*

**In place of this narration (played or read), you can have a leader or a youth give their testimony about Christ being the greatest example of all.*

Lighthouse in the Night

For solo voice, two part women's choir and piano

Arranged by
TYLER CASTLETON

Words and music by
JENNY PHILLIPS

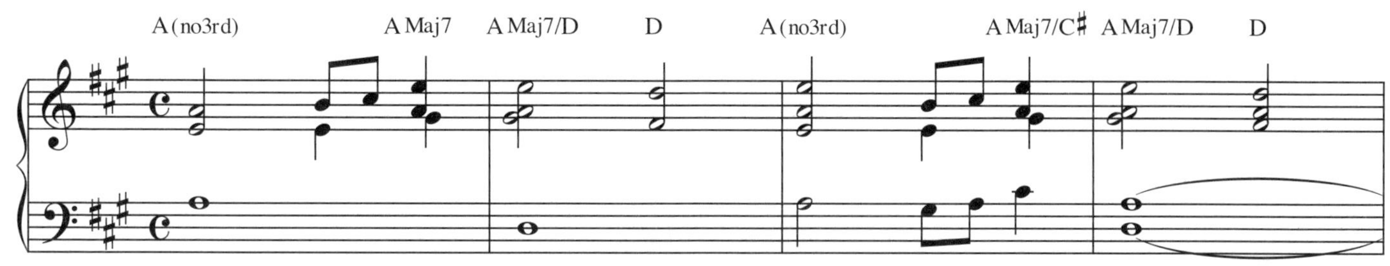

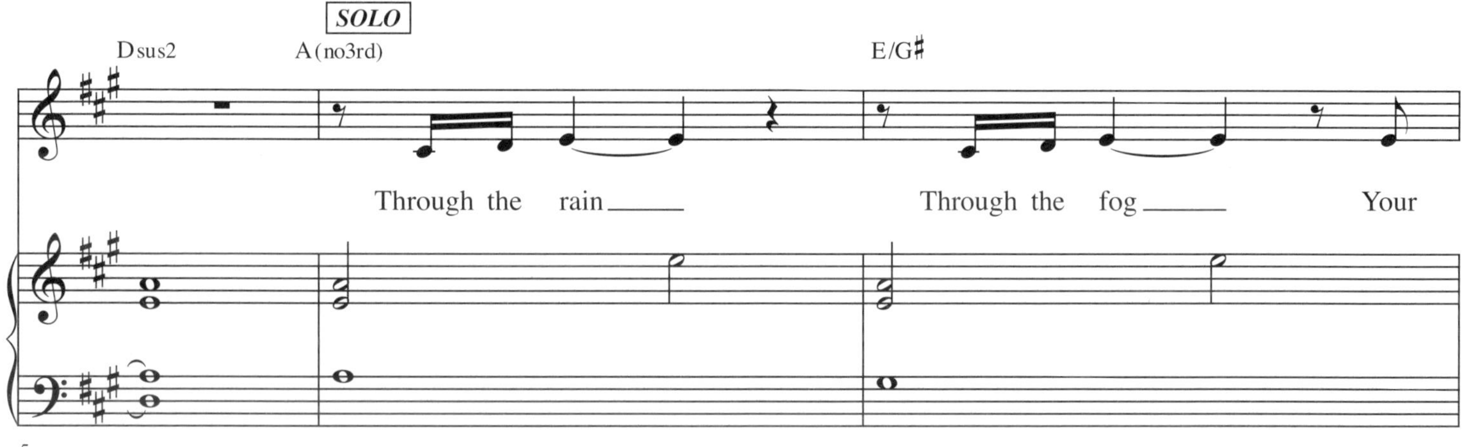

B min7 E sus4 A Maj7 F♯min7 D sus2 E sus4 E
flame of God in your life You stand tall a - bove the seas
12
A sus2 F♯min7 D sus2 E sus4 E A/C♯ B min9
Spread - ing light for all to see There are so ma - ny who can see your life
16
A add2/C♯ B min9 F♯min A Maj9/C♯
So man - y search - ing that will see you shine Your ex - am - ple steers them to
20
D Maj7 B min9 A A/C♯ D sus2♯4 D
Christ like a light - house in the night
23

A AMaj7/C♯ A(no3rd) AMaj7
Full of hope Full of peace how
27
Bmin7 Esus4 E Dsus2
bright your faith-ful- ness beams You make the way clear - er Lead-ing souls
3
31
Dadd2/F♯ Bmin7 Esus4 E
home a-gain You are re-mind-ing men of the way You
34
AMaj7 F♯min7 Dsus2 Esus4 E Aadd2 F♯min Dsus2 Esus4 E
stand tall a-bove the seas Spread - ing light for all to see
37

A/C♯
Bmin9
Aadd2/C♯
There are so ma - ny who can see your life
So man - y search - ing that will
41

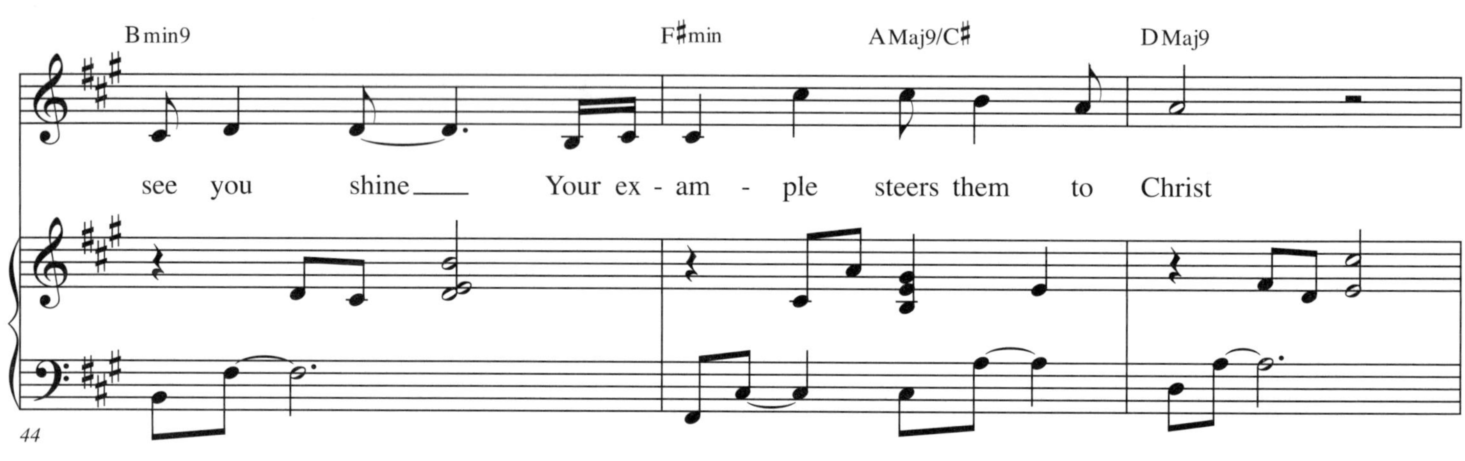
Bmin9
F♯min
AMaj9/C♯
DMaj9
see you shine
Your ex - am - ple steers them to Christ
44

Bmin7
E7sus4
DMaj9
like a light - house in the night
CHOIR
Through the rain and through the fog we're
47

Aadd2/C♯
DMaj9
reach - ing out to all the lost Through the rain and through the fog we're
49
AMaj9/C♯
Bmin7
reach - ing out to all the lost We're di - scip - les of Christ And
51
Esus4 E AMaj7 F♯min7 Dsus2 Esus4 E
He is our light We stand tall a - bove the seas
53
Asus2 F♯min Dsus2 Esus4 E A/C♯
spread - ing light for all to see There are so man - y who can
56

Bmin9
Aadd2/C♯
Bmin9
see our lives
So man - y search - ing who will see us shine
May our ex-
59
F♯min
AMaj9/C♯
DMaj9
Bmin9
am - ples steer them to Christ
Like a light - house in the night
62
A
A/C♯
Dsus2♯4
D
A
AMaj7/C♯
rit.
65
Dsus2♯4
D
A
68

Fit for His Kingdom

For solo female voice with optional male voice

Arranged by
TYLER CASTLETON

Words and music by
JENNY PHILLIPS and
TYLER CASTLETON

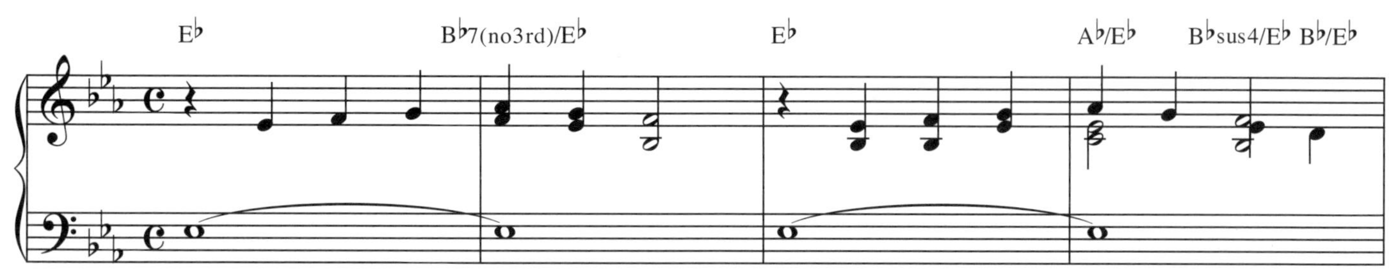

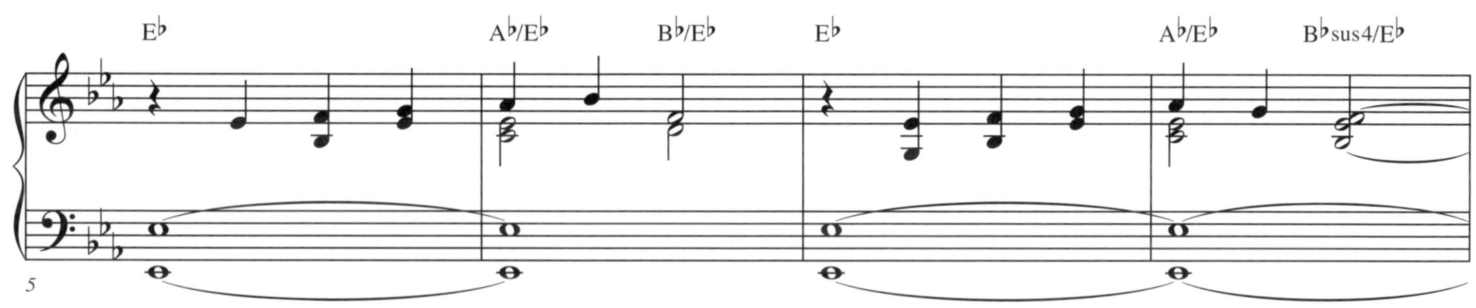

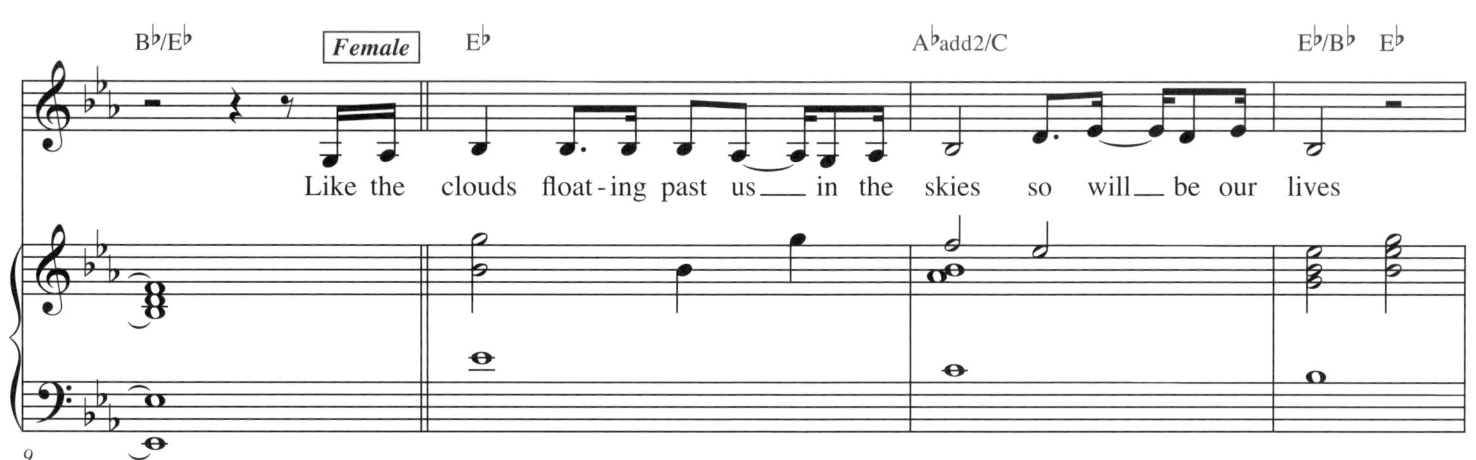

A♭add2/C E♭ E♭sus2 A♭/C E♭/B♭
We came here to be tried we came here to grow but
13
C min G min7 A♭add2 A♭sus2 E♭ B♭/D
we will come and go He waits for my re -
Male
waits my re -
17
C min B♭ A♭ B♭sus4 B♭ E♭ B♭/F
turn He waits for His child to come home I want to fight
turn He waits for His child
21

C min B♭ A♭ B♭sus4 B♭ F min C min/E♭
in this life___ for Him When I go home a -
I go home a -
25
B♭/D G min7 A♭add2 B♭7sus4 E♭
gain I want_ to be fit for His king - dom
gain I want_ to be___ More fit to
29
A♭/E♭ B♭/E♭ E♭ A♭/E♭ b sus4/E♭ B♭/E♭
He
see His face more wor - thy of His name
33

Female
E♭ A♭add2/C E♭/B♭ A♭add2/C
placed the sword of truth in my hands He trust ed me to stand I feel Him
37
E♭ A♭add2/C C min11 E♭/B♭ C min G min7/B♭
whis-per like the wind the val - ue of my life I am no - ble in His
whis-per like the wind no - ble in His
41
A♭sus2 E♭ B♭/E C min G min7/B♭
eyes He waits for my re - turn He waits for His
eyes waits my re - turn He waits for His
45

A♭sus2 B♭sus4 E♭ B♭/D C min G min7/B♭
child to come home I want to fight in this life for
B♭
child
49
A♭add2 B♭sus4 F min C min/E♭ B♭/D G min7
Him When I go home a - gain I want to
B♭
I go home a - gain I want to
53
A♭add2 B♭sus4 E♭ B♭7(no3rd)/E♭
be fit for His king - dom
be
57

E♭
A♭/E♭
B♭sus4/E♭
B♭/E♭
E♭
A♭/E♭
B♭/E♭
More fit to see His face
61
E♭
A♭/E♭
B♭sus4/E♭
B♭/E♭
E♭
more wor - thy of His name
rit.
65

Firm in the Faith

For solo female voice with women's choir

Arranged by
TYLER CASTLETON

Words and music by
JENNY PHILLIPS and
TYLER CASTLETON

Gsus2 D/F♯ G A sus4 A
hold-ing to who I am I am choos-ing my Fath-er's plan And
fol-low where-ev-er He leads trust-ing His way in all things He has
13
E min B min/D A/C♯ E min B/D♯ A/C♯ Gadd2/B
ev-ery-day I live I want to stand with Him Firm in the
called me to His side and I will live my life Firm in the
17
D A sus4 A E min B min7 A sus4 A
faith an-chored in truth sol-id in all that I do No turn-ing a-
faith
21
D A sus4 A E min B min A sus4 A
way no shad ow of doubt No storm has the pow-er to drag me down I'm a
25

B min
F♯min/A
G
D/F♯
E min
A 7sus4
alternate lower melody
wit - ness in these lat - ter days and I'm stand - ing firm in the faith
29
1.
B min
A
G
D/F♯
A/C♯
B min
F♯min
G
A sus4
A
32
D
2.
D (no3rd)
I am faith
36
Choir
D (no3rd)/C♯
B min7
Gsus2
Like Jo - seph, like Hy - rum Like Dan - iel in the li - on's den
40

D(no3rd) D(no3rd)/C# B min7 Gsus2 E min7
Like Mor-mon, like Am-mon Like Hel-a-man's young val-iant men
43
D(no3rd) D(no3rd)/C# B min7 Gsus2 Emin11
Like Es-ther, like Ne-phi Like all the saints who fol-lowed Christ
46
A sus4 Soloist D A sus4 A E min B min
Firm in the faith an-chored in truth sol-id in all that I
49
A sus4 A D A sus4 A E min B min
do No turn-ing a-way no shad-ow of doubt No storm has the pow-er to
53

A sus4
A
B min
F♯min
G
D/F♯
E min
A 7sus4
alternate lower melody
drag me down I'm a wit-ness in these lat-ter days and I'm stand-ing firm in the faith
57

B min
A
G
D/F♯
A/C♯
B min
F♯min
G
A sus4
A
61

D(no3rd)
65

Light Keeper

For solo female voice with unison women's choir

Arranged by
TYLER CASTLETON

Words and music by
JENNY PHILLIPS and
TYLER CASTLETON

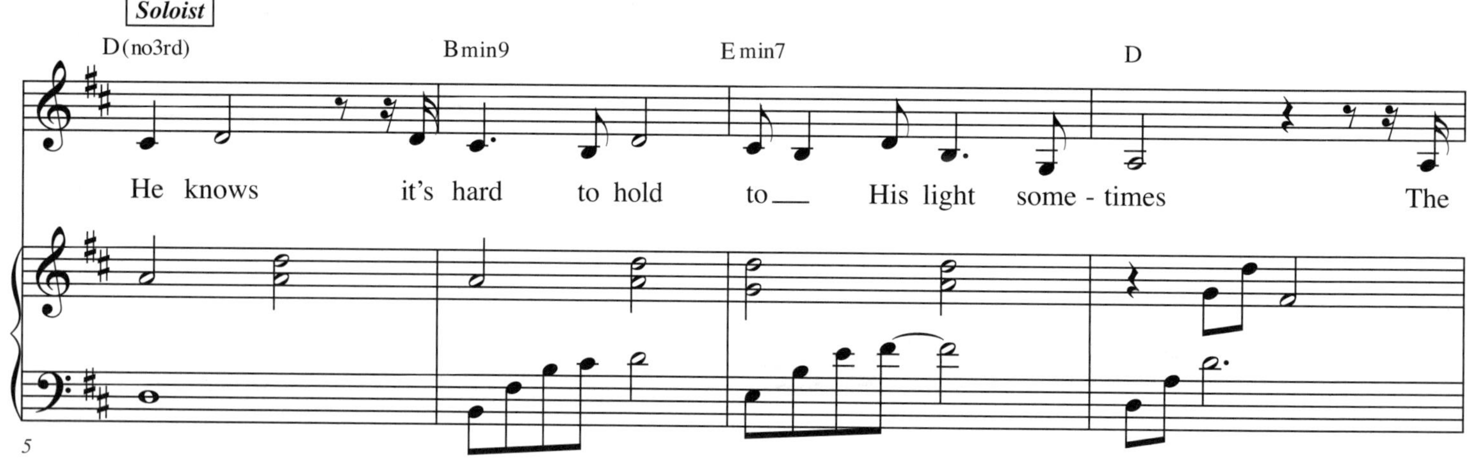

G Maj7/B
B min
Emin11
He'll help you shine— Light keep-er be strong Light keep-er walk
13
A sus4
A
B min
A/G
G
D
A sus4
A
on through the night— when all the world is tell-ing you it's not worth the fight hold
17
Emin7
Gsus2
D(no3rd)
G/D
D
Gsus2
on to your light— hold it tight light keep-er—
20
D(no3rd)
B min7
Emin11
Dsus4
D
You might feel— left be-hind when o - thers leave the light
25

D(no3rd)
B min7
Emin11
G
Oh how the Fath - er loves you He'll nev er leave your side
29

GMaj9
A
A/C♯
GMaj7/B
B min7
Emin11
He'll help you shine Light keep-er be strong Light keep-er walk
33

A sus4
A
B min
A/G
G
D
A sus4
A
on through the night when all the world is tell-ing you it's not worth the fight hold
37

Emin7 Gsus2 D(no3rd) D Bmin A/C♯
on to your light hold it tight light keep-er Oh how you
Choir
Oh how you
40
D Bmin F♯min Gadd2 Bmin F♯min
shine you are filled with the Fath - er's love You are wor - thy of His trust
shine you are filled with the Fath - er's love You are wor - thy of His trust
45
Soloist
Gadd2 D/F♯ Asus4 A GMaj7/B
Oh what beau - ti - ful light Light keep-er be
Oh what beau - ti - ful light
49

B min
Emin11
A sus4
A
strong Light keep-er walk on through the night when
53
B min
A/G
G
D
A sus4
A
E min7
all the world is tell-ing you it's not worth the fight hold on to your light hold it
56
Gsus2
D(no3rd)
G/D
D
D sus4
tight light keep - er
59
A sus4/D
G sus2
rit.
63

He Is the Way

Arranged by
TYLER CASTLETON

Words and music by
JENNY PHILLIPS

A sus4 D Emin11 A sus4 A
say He is the Way He is the Light He is Life No oth-er
19
D Emin11 A sus4 A B min
road No oth-er name has power to save I tes-ti-fy with
23
Emin11 D/F♯ Gadd2 A 7sus4 Dsus2
ev-ery breath I breathe with all my faith He is the Way
27
D sus4 D/F♯ G D/F♯ F Gadd2 A sus4 A A 7sus4 D(no3)
How bless-ed is His path How
31

Gadd2/B D/F♯ Gadd2 D(no3)
sweet it feels to me How I love the One ___ who leads If I could sound His ho-ly name and
36
Gadd2/B Emin7 D/F♯ Gadd2 A sus4 A A7sus4
kin-dle some-one's faith I would wear a - way ___ my life to ___ say He is the
40
D Emin11 A sus4 A D Emin11
Way He is the Light ___ He is Life No oth-er road No oth-er name has power to
44
A sus4 A B min Emin11 D/F♯
save A I tes-ti-fy ___ with ev-ery breath I breathe with all my
49

Gadd2 A7sus4 D(no3) Bmin11 Dadd2/A
faith He is the Way Light and life joy and peace
53
Emin11 A sus4 A Bmin11
liv - ing hope hands of mer - cy pow - er, growth
57
D/A Emin11 A sus4/G A sus4 Gadd2
truth and strength love and pro-gress good - ness grace He is the road He is the
slower
60
D/F♯ Emin11 D(no3)
path He is the Gate He is the Way
rit.
65

3

Hold Our Torches High

For two part women's choir with optional men's part

Arranged by
TYLER CASTLETON

Words and music by
JENNY PHILLIPS and
TYLER CASTLETON

E min7
Dadd2/F♯
E min7
and we can feel the pow - er of the Ho - ly Ghost We stand as wit - ness - es that
13
D/F♯
Gadd2
A sus4
A
D
all the world might know these things We will hold our torch - es
16
F♯min
E min7
A sus4
A
A/C♯
Gadd2/B
to the skies__ we will be ex - am - ples of His__ light We will live our lives with
19

Dadd2/F♯ Emin11 Dsus2/F♯
tes - ti - mo - ny He is the light we shine as we
23
Gadd2 A7sus4 D F♯min Gadd2
hold our torch - es high
27
Asus4 A D(no3rd) G/B B min
We live in a world full of dark - ness but we have know ledge of His great
31

Hold Our Torches High

Hold Our Torches High

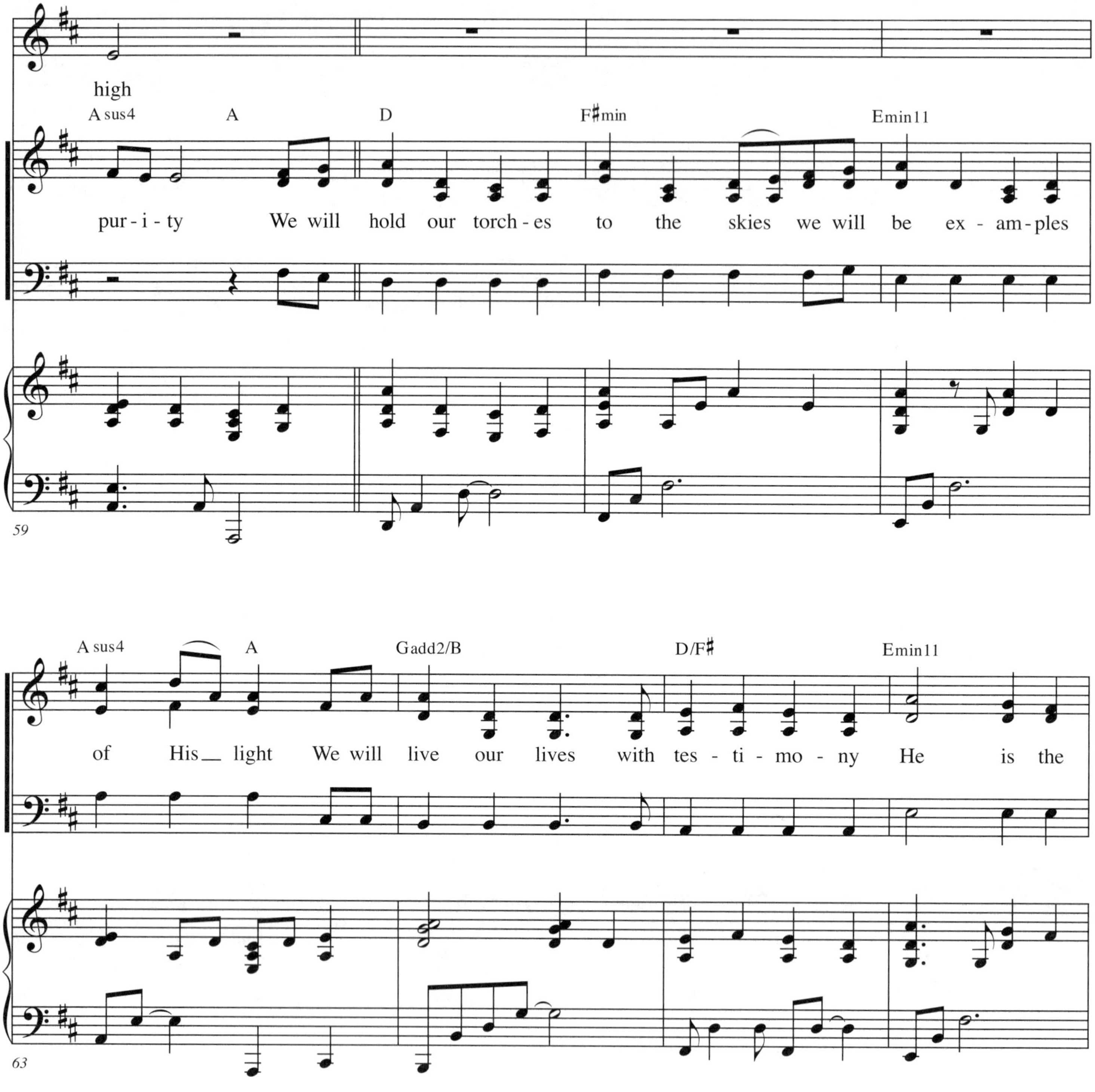

high

A sus4 A D F♯min Emin11

pur - i - ty We will hold our torch - es to the skies we will be ex - am - ples

59

Dadd2/F♯ Gadd2 A7sus4 B min A
light we shine as we hold our torch-es high We will
67
E min7 G Maj7 A sus4 D E min11
hold our torch - es high
D
71
D/F♯ G Maj7
rit.
75